SHE WATCHES WILD HORSES

Elisa Salasin

Finishing Line Press
Georgetown, Kentucky

SHE WATCHES WILD HORSES

For Sal

Publisher: Leah Huete de Maines
Editor: Christen Kincaid
Cover Art: Elisa Salasin
Author Photo: Elisa Salasin
Cover Design: Elizabeth Maines McCleavy

Order online: www.finishinglinepress.com
also available on amazon.com

Author inquiries and mail orders:
Finishing Line Press
PO Box 1626
Georgetown, Kentucky 40324
USA

Table of Contents

From the beginning I am told:

I want is never a good enough
reason for anything.

Words etched
into my ribs, words holding
an almost airless fire, a slow burn
husked hollow hunk of matter.

This is how my body becomes dust.

February 26

At midnight tomorrow I fly to Guadalajara, Mexico. I'll meet my sister, who will arrive from Texas, and together we'll collect Sal, our revolutionary poet uncle. He is in the late stages of lung cancer according to his Mexican neurosurgeon.

Sal is apparently nearly immobile and strung out on painkillers. We are to bring him home with us, barely 36 hours after arriving at his door. I don't want to sound crass; I'm not sure what to do with him when we return.

A neurosurgeon may not be the most reliable source for diagnosing lung cancer, but he tells us for sure it is—

Severe, really bad.

You don't want him to die in Mexico.

Come get him.

Come get him now.

Rosa Parks' Hair

There is a story I heard Alice Walker tell soon after Rosa Parks died. They were at some sort of dinner together and Alice Walker came across Parks in the women's restroom. These are Walker's words—

> *She suddenly took down her hair, and Rosa Parks had hair that came all the way down to her—you know, the lower back, and she quickly ran her fingers through it. I was just stunned. I had no idea. She then twisted it up again, and she put it the way you've seen her, you know, always with the little bun, very neat, and I said to her, "My goodness, what's all this, Miss Rosa?" And she looked at me, and she said, "Well, you know, I'm part Choctaw, and my hair was something that my husband dearly, dearly loved about me. He loved my hair." And she said, "And so, when he died, I put it up, and I never wear it down in public." Now there's a Rosa.*

> *So, you know, writers are just—we live by stealth, and so I immediately had this completely different image of this woman: the little, quiet seamstress sitting on the bus, even the activist who was so demure and so correct. And I thought, this woman, hallelujah, was with a man who loved her and loved her with her hair hanging down, and she loved him so much that when he died, she took that hair that he loved, and she put it up on her head, and she never let anyone else see it. Isn't that amazing?*

I've kept my soul wrapped up tight for my entire life,
hidden from all, even myself.
This was a way to control what got in and what got out.
Is a soul nurtured?
Can a soul grow?
Or is it just discovered?

When I think about this Rosa Parks story
I think about the various parts of me I've allowed to hang down,
whether that has been accepted, embraced,
loved in all its good and bad,
whether I am capable of doing that for myself,
accepting and embracing the living complexity. I want that for everyone.

This is where the journey begins.

Prose Poem for Sal

It wasn't until later when Bob Holman told me that Pedro Pietri died of stomach cancer on his flight from Mexico to New York that I began to perseverate about how we got you onto that airplane. Did I carry you from behind, holding up the weight of your body with my own, careful not to further break your broken back, or did you cling around my neck, my body your life preserver down that narrow airplane aisle. Does it matter? Somehow we carried you through the terminal and down the endless boarding tunnel to seat 9B. Amanda brought up the rear with all of the pillows and gear necessary for a dying poet's last journey.

It wasn't until later when Bob Holman told me that Pedro Pietri died on his flight from Mexico to New York that I remembered those moments with you in the men's room of the Guadalajara airport when you announced you finally had to take the shit you hadn't taken in weeks, and I brought you to the only stall, the one with no door, heaved you onto the toilet, and turned my head to allow the Mexican men that came in to pee their privacy while you had none. Your shit was a false alarm, but I wiped you nonetheless, for which the peeing Mexican men allowed us our privacy, and I worried for the remainder of the journey that the shit would arrive at 30,000 feet and what would I do then?

It wasn't until later when Bob Holman told me that Pedro Pietri died on his flight from Mexico to New York that I allowed myself to feel those stretches of silent terror when we thought you might already be dead. There you were in the middle bulkhead seat, slumped over the pile of pillows we'd placed in your lap because you could not sit upright, and it seemed like your breathing had slowed to its final stop. In those moments I debated with myself about what I'd do if it all ended over Mexico, over Arizona, Nevada, or in the long descent to SFO. Would I call for help? Or sit quietly until landing, until every passenger deplaned, before gently telling the flight attendants that we'd need more help than expected to remove you from their aircraft.

It wasn't until later when Bob Holman told me that Pedro Pietri died on his flight from Mexico to New York that the words of the Mexican doctor came back to me: *Por supuesto they'll let him on the airplane! This is México!*

It will be hours until the buxom blond Highland Hospital ER doctor will look into your hungry eyes and announce that you have a tumor the size of a baseball in your chest, to which you will respond: *I was a great poet. Just remember, I was a great poet.* But for now, I slip you extra pain pastillas, I sigh into this caesura and order two more shots of free airplane tequila (*This is México!*). Both for me.

March 6

We have moved Sal to a skilled nursing facility, brought in hospice care, tripled the pain meds, and delivered a bag-full of delicious looking medical marijuana bon bons. Sal is high as a kite and in heaven, or at least that's his report—*I'm in heaven, HEAVEN!!* Seeing as yesterday he said he was in hell (*HELL!!*), I'd call it an improvement.

Sal had been self-medicating in Mexico, both with methadone pastillas as well as with his rather large stash of weed. When we rescued him from his apartment floor, the bag of marijuana was one of the items that we left behind, right where it had been stored next to his mattress. We weren't about to carry a dying man and his illegal substances across the border.

In any case, Sal is thrilled with the new developments (or as thrilled as one might be in his situation)—so much so that he asked his nurse to marry him, while also teaching her the first two lines of the Dao De Jing in Mandarin. True, at the point of the proposal he was pretty far gone, and it came out a mixture of Mandarin, Spanish and English. Whatever... my uncle was in heaven for the moment and succeeded in getting the nurse to promise to visit him on her day off.

March 8

Sal cried today. His pain meds stabilized, meaning his mind was free to wrap itself around the reality of what was happening to him. He knew he would die. Soon.

Yesterday he asked me to contact just one person—out of a whole lifetime, just one person—a poet friend from New York with whom he'd collaborated (and competed against) over the years. This morning I spoke with Bob on the phone. He was dumbstruck to hear about Sal's condition and wrote that my uncle is one of "earth's ferocious characters," who had beat back the system again and again. This is the comment that made Sal cry—the only tears he has shown throughout the past crazy week of returning to the US and fully accepting his diagnosis. At first, he kept saying that he's not ferocious, and his habit of trying to beat back the fucking system is one of his only regrets, that he wishes he had never made life so hard for himself. However, by the end of the conversation, he was feeling rather proud to be called one of the earth's ferocious characters and was sharing it with anyone that entered the room, including the Tibetan nurse's aide Tenzin, who didn't quite know what to make of it all.

I think that his breakdown today was a positive thing. I sat and listened, let him cry, and let him tell me stories about the Poetry Project scene, about the "fucking academic poets" that screwed him over and don't know a goddamn thing about poetry anyway. I let him rant and rave, and then talk about things that he loved. At one point, maybe 15 years ago, he abandoned New York for Seattle. He talked at length about kayaking in Puget Sound, and the peace that brought to him. Still, though, the writing... He seems to desperately need to know that his writing was important to someone in this world. I'm working on having other folks from his past send him messages along those lines.

After the ferocious breakdown a nurse and I cooperated to give Sal a shave, to bring back the carefully tended "Greco-Roman goatee" that had fallen into overgrown disrepair during the past few months. By the end he looked downright handsome, and very pleased he wouldn't be scaring my kids, both of whom will tomorrow meet the great uncle they never knew they had before last week.

Did I mention that before going to Mexico to retrieve him, I hadn't seen Sal in 11 years? That he was essentially a stranger to me?

March 10

And what's the point
to all these gettings-up-in-the-morning
and goings-to-bed-at-night?
All these rubbings-off, -on and -into?
All these eatings-of-meals, all these
puttings-of-legs-into-pants,
all these rooms?
Nothing is real and it's all dancing, right?
I'm gone but my voice wheedles on.

The drugs they gave me yesterday are finally working, and I can think through the pain, I can see more clearly what this future holds for me, and I want out: *Fate and too many painkillers, my favorite combination.*

Good morning! God loves you! I love you! Have a nice day.

There's the old woman from two rooms down... Judging by that blank stare she's blind. Here she is with her fucking daily mantra. She'll repeat the same goddamn thing at every door on the hallway, wheeling herself along, and then she'll do it again this afternoon, and again tonight. Once I would've told her that *if God exists, I'm really fucked*, but now it appears I'm fucked regardless. I can't wipe my own shit or lift my arm to feed myself. I'm warehoused for $10,000 a month. I will never finish off my tele-novela narco-trafficking opera, much less focus on even one poem in the Rilke book Elisa brought for me. I'm fucked.

"You always hurt the one you love."
Like that? Here's another:
"You never know what you have until you lose it."
Isn't that terrific? These are
pearls from the mouths of
Fashion Institute of Technology babes.
They talk just like that I swear.

Good morning! God loves you! I love you! Have a nice day.

I have a plan. Elisa will help me. She can get a room in a motel, one of those side-of-the-highway joints, cheap. She can sign me out of my 10-grand hell, say that I'll be visiting her for dinner, and then deposit me in the motel along with a bottle of pills and plenty of weed. She can tell these people that I wandered off from dinner, she doesn't know where. I haven't figured out how she'll explain my wandering, when I can't even move six inches up the bed without her, but I know she will find a way. She's the smart one.

Good morning! God loves you! I love you! Have a nice day.

Maybe I should've kept quiet. Elisa is patient, but I see the tenseness in her body. She brushes tears from the edges of her eyes and thinks I don't notice. She talks about Oregon, she googles hospice, she says she doesn't know if she can do this for me. I tell her: *This is no time to be gloomy, we're all dying.* She laughs, for a moment at least, but I don't think she's down with the plan.

Good morning! God loves you! I love you! Have a nice day.

Elisa takes my hands and tells me to look her in the eyes. She leans in and quietly, so quietly whispers that she loves me and that the razor blade from yesterday's shave is in the bedside drawer. I'm not sure I can get to that drawer, but it's probably easier than getting to a motel. I tell her *thank you, thank you, thankyousoverymuch thank you.* I've got this at least, just two feet away, I've got this, and now I can sleep.

> *But it wasn't always like that.*
> *Once I was feeding five-yen coins*
> *into a Japanese pay phone in the*
> *pouring rain. Sitting up,*
> *watching the red dot of a cigarette,*
> *thinking how nothing in Japan*
> *is far from the sound of water.*

Good morning! God loves you! I love you! Have a nice day.

(Excerpts from Sal Salasin, Optima Suavidad, Green Bean Press)

March 11

The structure of the current situation with my uncle is a little complicated. He's in a skilled nursing facility, but the nurses and doctors there basically just do caretaking and administer the meds.

Then, there's the whole team of hospice-care people: doctor, nurse, social worker, volunteers. Their services are contracted out. They come in and do their assessments, set up the pain relief schedule and provide some level of end-of-life emotional support. Given that they work for a big corporation, I was a bit skeptical about what we could expect from Hospice Inc., but I'm pleased to say that they are quite wonderful.

The nurse that visits Sal almost daily is present and compassionate, really listens to him, and has taken his desire to end his life sooner rather than later very seriously. Luckily, she's talked him out of a few of the riskier schemes that he had running through his head, and we've now set a plan for moving forward. A plan he is in charge of beginning when he decides that he is ready. At that time, he is going to stop eating and taking in liquids, and his meds will be increased until he's essentially tuned out mentally. It could run anywhere between a few days to a few weeks for him to pass, but all agreed it was the best of the possible options. Earlier today he was set to begin, but then the nurse upped the meds, and lo and behold it made him feel pretty damn good. He decided that the time has not come yet. We're just going with it as he calls it. He says he doesn't want to be a drain on resources and doesn't want to be a burden.

When I look at the state of my life right now, I can see how spending this time caring for him could be perceived as a burden—I'm often there for five or more hours a day, I'm behind in my job, wandering in my life, I miss my children, and have spent a not inconsiderable amount of time and money in providing for his general needs and comfort in whatever ways that I am able. However, as I thought about this all today, I realized that I find this whole experience to be much more of a privilege than a burden.

A friend recently wrote to me that he sees one of our highest callings as humans is to help others in their transition out of this world. I'm not sure I ever would have understood that before now. In some ways it has been the purest form of interaction I've ever had. There is nothing trivial, nothing filler, nothing that is not essential. Sal has been processing his life, in some ways learning how to live. Kind of ironic—learning how to live when one has such limited time remaining. Being there with him feels out of time, yet so very numbered. I'm not sure this makes any sense, but many things now are both senseless and yet very clear to me.

Perhaps I am learning how to live as well.

Today Sal told me that he didn't want me losing out on my own life through spending time with him. I replied that I am honored to be there, and that was the truth. The relief on his face was palpable, and he flat out said, "Good. Because you are really important to me now."

One of the surprises he's experiencing is that he wants company, wants to be around people and wants to talk—after a lifetime of being solitary, he wants people, and this discovery seems to delight him. I wish there were more people around that had time to come and listen to his stories, to sit and just be with him.

Not because I don't want that responsibility, but rather because it is a truly special experience. It is a privilege.

March 12

Today my uncle asked me to send a message to a woman named Whitney that he fell in love with several years ago. She was almost 40 years younger, and they apparently had an intense internet relationship, never consummated. Sal gave me the password for his email account so that I could find her address.

I went in and retrieved it, wrote out his very personal and heartfelt goodbye to her, and sent it off.

Turns out I got the wrong Whitney. Fuck.

I have not heard back from the mistaken Whitney who just received a message from her dying former union colleague that she was the love of his life.

March 13—Still Life

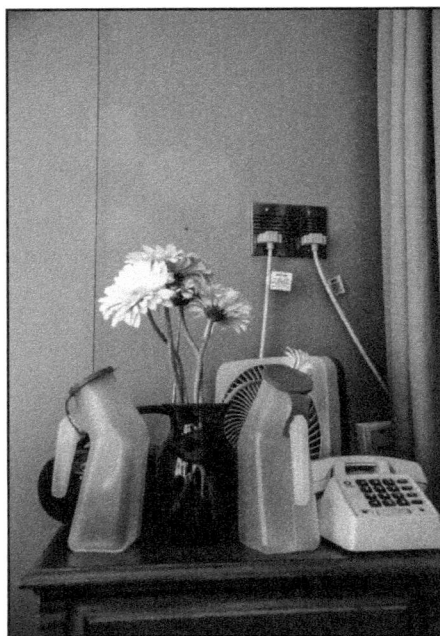

He's still alive.

The mistaken Whitney from yesterday's misdirected email wrote a very gracious note back. The correct Whitney replied saying that she is going to write a letter to Sal, but it has yet to materialize. If she doesn't deliver the goods, it'll break his heart, so she damn well better write something.

Sal finally gave me permission to send news out to a few other poetry folks. A message was posted to a listserv, suggesting that people send poems of a wry or humorous bent (very much in keeping with Sal's work). I'm starting to get missives from poets around the country. I know this will make Sal happy.

Sometime this weekend I'm aiming for writing about something different. I'd like that. But I'd also like a foot massage, and to sleep in until noon. I'm not likely to get any of it, so at least I can aim for writing about a new topic and maybe some camera and creative time. We shall see what the weekend brings.

March 16—Guns & Monks

Today I read Sal two letters—one from his young internet love, and the other from the ex-wife that he hadn't spoken to in thirty years. They both made him cry with longing and regret. Many notes, poems, and letters are coming in now. I've been printing them all and putting them in a binder that people who visit can read to him (mostly me, as he doesn't have anyone else other than a social worker). He is proud to be getting so many messages and poems from around the world—some from people that never met him but knew his work—but this pride is mixed with sorrow about running away from everyone for so long. Now, he doesn't want to run. Many, many tears today. His anguish is incredibly deep.

Earlier I spoke on the phone with the old friend that is in possession of my Buddhist & pacifist uncle's AK-47. Well, Sal isn't the actual owner, because the FBI wouldn't let him take possession due to the felony pot-bust back in '68, so his friend and union coworker, Chuck, is the official owner of Sal's high-power firearm. There is a long and complicated story that goes with the AK-47, which ends with Sal being run out of the county where he was living prior to going to Mexico. Chuck wanted to fill me in on the true story of the gun, just in case others presented the sensationalist but incorrect telling that paints Sal as a potential murderer. Chuck said something about Sal wanting to hunt bears in Alaska.

Sal now has a Tibetan monk (in Nepal) praying for him, the un-unionized workers in Heaven standing at the ready for his organizing skills, and another old love offering to pay his medical bills, since she has reportedly lived frugally all her life and has quite a "substantial" sum saved away. Not bad for a reclusive poet.

I am tired.
Fine cracks spread across my body.

Strain seeps to my outside.
I am parched.

But I do not crack.
I hold together.

Choiceless, I hold together.
Tired, I hold together

Monks offer prayers
if only they can be found.

March 17—Cancer

My uncle might as well have been a stranger a few weeks ago, or virtually so. He was the one that got me high in my parent's basement as a teenager, that took me out for Chinese food once or twice in NYC (always ordering in perfect Mandarin), came to my wedding (but cut out early without saying goodbye), and sent amusing and well-written emails from Mexico. Not a complete stranger…

Then it all changed. My sister and I went to Guadalajara, picked him up off his floor, and carried him back to California.

Now, I sit by his side, hours every day. I hold his hand as he sleeps, waking up every few minutes to yell, "Help! Help me! Ayudame por favor!" I check on his pain meds, I have care conferences in sterile meeting rooms, I cover him as he writhes naked on his bed because every time we put a gown, or clothing, or a diaper on his body, he rips them off. I watch as the tumor in his chest begins to swell and discolor his skin. I feed him pints of double chocolate chip ice cream, read him letters and poems, try to get him to wear his oxygen tubes, and listen, listen, listen as he free-associates his way toward death. I've become as much his wife/lover/mother as his niece.

Yesterday was bad. Really bad. His pain was out of control, and his agony was non-stop. It seems to finally be managed again, for the moment, though he's currently under 24-hour watch to make sure.

Half the time he can't tell you what state or city he's in, and calls me by the wrong name, but can sing revolutionary songs to the word and remember the name of his kindergarten teacher. And on and on and on—a co-mingling of English, Spanish, Mandarin, Chinese history, Mexican gangsters, little boy calling for his mother, union organizing, poetry rants, and endless requests to be moved 6-inches up the bed because he can't do it himself.

His nurse says that he has "brain mets" and it sounds like little creatures crawling around inside his head, grabbing on to the ends of neurons and swinging back and forth like in the circus. Like a brain carnival, only there's nothing festive about it. I must ask what brain mets means, just to be sure.

I want to believe that whatever I learn from this experience will carry me forward towards the much-needed break-through in my own life. I cannot continue to wait, cannot delay my living. None of us can.

A Typical Interaction from Our Day

Get me out of here, get me out of here!

> Where are we?

We're in the Arizona desert, and you need to get gas in the car to get us out of here!

> Why are we in the desert?

We're here to organize workers, and you've got to me out of here NOW! Get gas! We've got to leave! Just get me to that long, dark tunnel and we'll be okay. Do it now! Help ME!!

> You can go to that tunnel. You can take yourself there. Just close your eyes and let go. You can do that. I'm here with you, but you can go to that tunnel.

No, NO!! You don't understand! You've got to get gas in the car. I need you to do this for me. They're coming for me, and I need you to get me out of here. I'm dying here!

> Yes. You are. You are dying here, with me. Close your eyes. It is time to sleep. I love you.

Okay. I'll sleep. Yes.
Good-night, and thank you, thank you, thank you so so much.

> Thank you so very much.

Angels and Shakespeare

It has been an intense week,
after an intense three weeks.

These days have been the most difficult.
I'd been by his side the entire day, holding his hand, stroking his forehead,
trying to help him be calm and let go.

For the past several days he hadn't been in much, if any, physical pain.
However, the psychic pain, the knowledge that he was at death's door and not
ready to go through, did not allow him much peace.

During the time that he was awake, Sal would thrash, he would rant
incoherently, he'd try to climb out the window, off the bed, he'd moan and
sweat and repeat his endless mantra of, "Please, por favor, help me! Help me
please, help me!"

In spite of his condition, he was still strong, really strong, and even today it
took me and at least one other person to hold him back and keep him safe.

Then, two things happened.
Both magical.

This morning, as we were trying to calm him, one of the nurses mentioned
we should turn on the CD in the little portable player I'd brought him. She
mentioned that he particularly loved the second track.

What CD?

I'd brought the player for the radio, and though I'd meant to bring in some
music, I'd forgotten to do so. Sure enough, there was an unmarked disc in the
player. Track 2 was a hauntingly beautiful folk song in Spanish about death.
As Sal listened, his body untensed, and he was able to fall asleep. We played
the track again and again, because each time it ended he'd get restless. I asked
around to several of the people that would likely have brought it to him (there
really aren't very many possibilities), and none had any idea where it came
from. I took to calling it the CD *Sent By Angels*. I suppose I could probably ask
around some more, but I rather like my current explanation.

In the afternoon he experienced another attack of panic and anxiety. He talked
about wanting hot and cold, light and dark, about the water rising around

him. He invoked Vesuvius, said he wanted to die on top of a volcano. He curled his body like that of a baby—legs in the air, arms moving about trying to find something to grasp, something to cling to as he was trying to cling to life.

At one point amidst the movement and internal/external chaos, Sal called out for Shakespeare. He wanted to know when Shakespeare would be arriving. I held his hand and said that Shakespeare was on his way. He asked if Shakespeare would be taking him upstairs. I said that yes, Shakespeare was coming to take him upstairs, and once there they'd meet up with Neruda and Cervantes and Lorca, and they'd talk about poetry together. I told him there were un-unionized workers that needed to be organized, and innumerable poets waiting for him in heaven, and that Shakespeare would be arriving very soon to guide him there.

Sal began repeating, *Shakespeare is coming... Shakespeare is coming. He's coming soon...* As he did, his body uncurled, and he fell into a quiet sleep.

I sat holding my hand over his heart, whispering that Shakespeare would be there before too long, that we all love him, but that he was free to go. It was the most peaceful sleep I'd seen in days, so I left him in the care of his continuous-care nurse, an incredibly gentle and perceptive Pakistani man named Erfan.

It is March 19th, 2009. At 6:20 this evening my uncle died.

He had woken up briefly, and Erfan held him as he took his last breath.

Erfan later told me that literally moments before Sal died, several items fell off of the bedside table. Erfan picked them up and put them back, but as soon as he turned around they were inexplicably knocked on the floor again. No one had touched them. They were sturdy things, not prone to falling on their own.

Shakespeare had indeed arrived.

St. Diego

A friend sends me a poem with the following lines:

There are many kinds of people in the world,
but there are only two kinds of people in the world:
those who've helped a person die
and those who haven't.

(Night Eats the Last of It, Nancy Krygowski, from *Velocity*, University of Pittsburgh Press)

I've been lonely. In some senses that loneliness is okay, as I'm learning to be with myself in new and I believe important ways.

Tomorrow I fly to San Diego for two nights. At this point I really don't want to be out of town again. Time with my children has been too precious lately, and too little. However, there will be friends there, people that make me laugh and remember that I am smart and have something to say in this world. That'll be good.

The school buses are gathering outside her childhood home where she, simultaneously child and adult, rushes to grab lunches, shoes, backpacks for her children. She knows she is late, maybe too late, and runs out the front door empty-handed into the center of the lumbering flotilla of Glossy Yellow. Each bus, the same as the next, yet she knows they all will go to different schools, but not which schools, or where the schools are. Or when the bus she needs will leave, or if it has already left. Frozen amidst the circling fleet, she watches as one by one each bus slowly drives away, empty of passengers, until she stands alone in the street, hybrid child and adult, undisturbed by all that she does not know or might have missed.

Low Tide

I stand on sand hard and wet—
wide beach, vast water-washed
plain scrubbed by wind
punctured by rocks worn
to round, hundreds of half-
buried seaside spheres

their fractured skins like spider
web bound orbs rasped by dogged
sun, by wave after insistent
wave & I wonder if their fissures
will hold through the oncoming
storms. This fragile stasis (rock-wind-

tide-sun) versus my headstrong
desire to find gold in the darkest
blue. Kneeling in the sand I dig
one cleaved rock
from its siliceous nest—
in a singular motion I pry and lift

as surface crumbles away, as rock
skin and gut release leaving behind
a tiny seashell core, now cupped
in my palm: this bared-

heart koan

fray of my human longing.

She wanders in darkness, at night, in cities. There are companions along the way, but she doesn't know who they are. On this trip she senses her goal but cannot name it. She knows the only way to get to this unnamable place is crossing the campus of a large school or summiting a long hill to go around. All the school gates are locked. She hesitates, not wanting to make the steep climb in the dark, as she has already been walking and walking for years and is bone-tired: if she can just get to the top of the hill, the rest of the way will be easier, she thinks as she imagines herself flying down the other side, weightless, free. She knows that life doesn't work as in dreams, but nonetheless begins the climb.

Scattering Liminal

In several hours I'm going to get on the Staten Island Ferry and scatter my uncle's ashes, with the help and company of several of Sal's poet friends. The other day, carrying the heavy box of cremation-remains up to NYC on the train, the gravity of what I'm doing hit me. I was sitting in a whirlpool of train station sounds: screeching brakes, construction noises, birds singing in the eves of the platform...

and I burst out crying.

I am in an in-between space, and tired of in-between spaces. So, I'm working on getting myself out of these spaces, these waiting zones, these states of mind where I feel like once x, y, or z happens I'll be able to move ahead with the "real" work I aspire towards. I'm trying to work with now rather than when/if—not always so easy to do, but the balance is shifting. I want to move out of in-between spaces.

I'm full of emotion—about Sal's life and about my own. I'm also nervous about how we're going to pull this off. You are supposed to get a permit for scattering ashes (which I didn't bother to do), so my next update may be coming from jail.

The Brilliant Mr. Salasin*

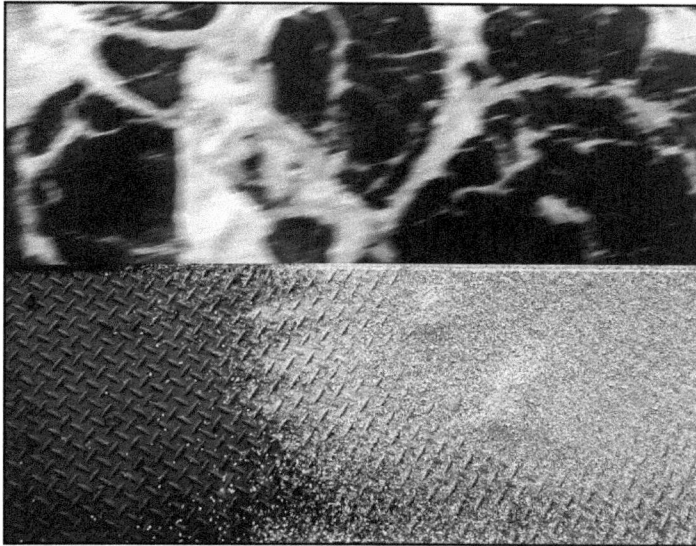

The brilliant Mr. Salasin—who likes cats.
His longtime princess and consort buys him lunch.
He is devilishly fond of her
and she seems fond enough of him.
Scatter my ashes from the Staten Island ferry.
Everyone has chosen to live here so this place
must be someplace special.
Every Monday has a Friday and
time heals everything too damn well.
The text is illegible
but I can't tear myself away. No waiting. Never a line.
I'm thirty-six
and all I know for sure is that it snows on the East River
all night.
Not many notice.
I have to ask myself
how can all this weightlessness survive.

*Sal Salasin, from *Stepping Out of the Plane Under the Protection of the Army*,
Another Chicago Press

She has lost everything, all her possessions, her books, her papers, her car and home, all physical evidence of her living, gone. She has lost everything, except for a dead cell phone and her children.

It is catharsis, and she buys strawberry ice pops from the vendor on the shore, a necessary treat after the harrowing journey.

Moments before she had scrambled her son and daughter to the safety of this sand, this beach, and they watched their sailboat, already missing its bow, swept out into the sea and destroyed, along with houses, massive buildings, an entire land swallowed by the black heaving mountains of water that still glimmer in the moonlight, a terrifying beauty. She is surprised at the calm strength that allowed her to pull the broken vessel ashore. Alone with her children, out on the water in a boat that she could not steer nor control, setting sail to an unknown destination in spite of the ominous clouds on the horizon.

She should have understood the danger. A good mother, a safe mother, would have known better. But she was tired of wandering. She was ready to leave.

She knew there would not be a map.

Happiness

My toddler son vomits strawberries
onto the slick marble floor & my daughter
cries she won't be able to hold her pee
through the snaking line for the one toilet.
Sweat pools and itches under my breasts
& the echo inside my head insists:
when in Italy, *I should be happy.*

I am trapped in the Florence airport
boarding lounge for unknown hours
and I cannot stop watching them:
the Italian woman and her husband.

In the swirl of overbooked flight delays
I stare as I strain to hear staccato
announcements in a language I do not
understand. I thought it all would make sense
by now. By now I thought I would know more.

The Italian woman and her husband:
haloed in my gaze she cradles his head
in her lap, she strokes his hairline, feathered
fingers a whisper and a private laugh
as another cancellation crackles
and he leans into her chest with a sigh.
They close their eyes to wait, their own still point
in the swirl of heat-frayed tourists.

I am happy. I want to believe.
This I thought I would understand by now.

I pull my bra up to catch the sweat.
I search for wipes to clean the floor. I push
misgivings into my overstuffed back-
pack & I try, I try to smile my way back home.

There is so much that I love
but there is even more that I want.

I am happy, I tell myself, I am—
Yet I cannot stop watching them:
the Italian woman and her husband.

Postscript

I searched New York for the right receptacle to hold a small amount of Sal's ashes that I wanted to preserve. The flea market at 25th and 7th Ave. yielded the perfect container—a round, wooden box approximately 4 inches in diameter that came from near Afghanistan/Pakistan and was supposedly 150 years old. I bought it from the crusty Brit antiques-gent who was touched by my expressed reason for needing a small box with a tight-fitting lid. He was close to Sal's age and shared that he hoped to meet his own end by climbing aboard his 50ft. yacht (which he'd had yet to acquire), alone, and sailing straight into the perfect storm. It was a beautifully profound 5-minute exchange on mortality and dreams, and he sold me the box for only $15.

When it came time to separate the large bag of remains, I divided it up as best I could between four Chinese food take-out containers. The choice of take-out boxes seemed in questionable taste, but all involved agreed that it was perfect and would have made Sal very pleased. The red wooden box got the last handful or two.

The poets and I found each other at the appointed time. We shared a beer and stories on the trip over to Staten Island, and then on the way back to Manhattan were blessed with an empty back of the boat. We were able to take our time and send Sal into the air and water with appropriate goodbyes. When a pile of the cremains didn't quite make it off the side of the boat, we decided that was fitting as well. "Sal would've approved," was the motto for the evening.

The weather was perfect, the sun low in the sky, and we read aloud from Sal's work, and from Shakespeare. At one point a couple of teenagers wandered out to the back and I simply pointed towards the breeze and said, "That's my uncle."

Maybe everything involved with the celebration of Sal's life went a little too perfectly. Because then... I lost the wooden box. I'm not sure how it happened. I distinctly remember packing it when I was preparing for my return trip to DC, but when I arrived it was gone. I've searched every possible bag and pocket. I've called and emailed the hotel where I must have left it. Nothing.

I'm disappointed but will let this go just as we let the rest of the ashes sail into the wind. In a way it isn't surprising. I carried him so far—from one country to another, through to the other side of life, and then across the United States. We took two plane trips, a train trip, more car trips than I can count, a boat trip. We navigated both the NYC Pride Parade and the subway (the existence of the former making the latter a much longer than necessary trip). And yesterday the Staten Island ferry crashed... If next I hear that the Washington Square Hotel burns down, I'll really suspect that something unexplainable is going on. Maybe Sal just wanted to stay in New York. All of him.

Azul

There's a walk that I've been taking for the past ten years. I go out my front door, and up the hill into increasingly wealthy residential neighborhoods. I love the route, but not for the fancy houses, rather the well-worn path traveled so many times by my feet, the serenity within an urban space, the occasional funky details, and otherworldly outcroppings. It is truly another dimension just up the hill, at least in my own mind. I like to walk, breathe, be inside my head, and observe.

One particular house, well-sequestered behind a large fence, has always intrigued me. It used to be a gorgeous shade of blue and had a sign on the fence that said, *Casa Azul*. I loved the visual shock of rounding the corner to see that blue shimmering within the green of the trees surrounding it. At some point the house changed owners and within a few months was repainted brown. I guess it still looks good—a deep, rich brown, but not the same as that blue. The *Casa Azul* sign still hangs in front, and a tiny blue buddha sits next to the entrance gate, now bearing the weight of being the only azul part of Casa Azul.

A few months ago, I learned Alice Walker lives in that house.

On Sunday, Mother's Day, I very consciously walked past. As I did, I remembered words that I wrote down when I heard her speak several years ago:

I have fallen in love with the imagination. And if you fall in love with the imagination, you understand that it is a free spirit. It will go anywhere, do anything. So your job is to find trustworthy companions and co-creators... That's really it.

It was a good walk.

Storage of the Dead

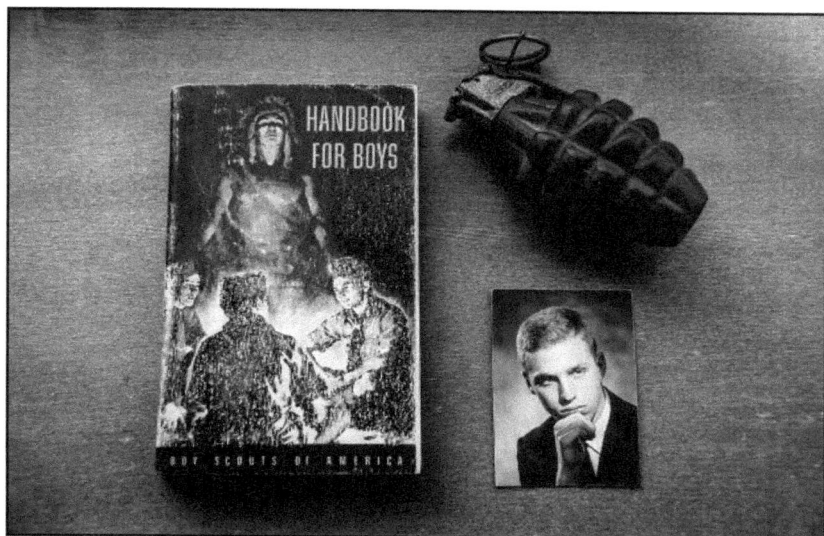

When Sal deposited most of his possessions and memories in a Seattle storage unit, I'm sure the last thing on his mind was that his nieces would someday be handling every one of them, one by one. Every last one of them.

Like his ashes, Sal's belongings are hitting the wind and infiltrating their way into the world. We made one especially wonderful used bookstore exceedingly happy, donated the Chinese history and Marxism to the University of Seattle, and distributed two cases of Sal's published poetry books across the city (bus stops, cafes, free newspaper boxes, and anywhere else that might be conducive to the surprise discovery of poetry).

All in two rainy days.

I kept much: the hand grenade, the poetry books by others, the antique Chinese waterpipes, and a most-excellent pair of black boots in men's size 10 and a half, too big for me but someone will get them. My sister got the samurai sword. We had a west coast Chinese dinner with Sal's union friends, who genuinely loved his crusty and bloated ego.

They get to keep the AK-47.

Murmuration

I cannot forget the cadence
of his thank yous
they come back to me like a lullaby
a chant for life
like a long cool drink, a sigh
an exhale, the chorus
of our own special song.

I cannot rid myself of deep
bone gratitude that arrives
on a frequency heard by those
on this earth that do not ask
if a dying man said thank you.

Did he say thank you?

I cannot answer.
I cannot speak.

I cannot tell of my poet uncle,
tumor swelling chest with limbs turned useless
his once man-body now stained with urine and open sores.

I cannot explain the cancer, the waning life I lifted
Into the dilapidated Guadalajara taxi broken
passenger seat that won't stay upright but that's ok
because neither will Sal's broken body.

I cannot tell of kindness, that driver
maneuvering cobblestone streets with tenderness
of last rites because each bump in the road shakes bones
rattles tumors each sudden stop a shotgun
of pain, a guttural moan, a potential death.

I cannot tell of my hesitancy
to reach forward from the back seat
to rest my hand ever so gently
on my uncle's one tumorless shoulder
not wanting to add to agony—
but I do reach I do say
I am here.

That is all.
I am here.

I cannot tell of that moment
when Sal lifted his fingers to mine
of how he brushed my skin
with wonder and the thirst
of someone that has not touched love
for months for years and who knows
that there is not much touching left.

I cannot express that under my hands
I feel Sal's breathing lengthen & slow
with whispered thank yous again
and again: *Thank you, thank you, thank you*
thankyouthankyou, thank you so very much,
thank you. (helpme! ¡ayudame!)
oh god. thank you. Over and again

I cannot yet say this out loud:
Show me how not to be afraid.
Show me that I exist to gleam
like the sinewy stream that flows
down this mountainside show me
that I can rise to the symphony
of my uncle's thank yous. Show me
that I can love as gracefully
as those wheeling and diving words—

I cannot—I want to—but I cannot translate:
Starlings murmur, lovers murmur
and Sal murmurs in and out
of the final days of his life: Thank you thank you
each thank you rising with the murmuration of poet voices
that murmur this is how to live into past into future:
murmur of love

lost: of a union that will not survive:
murmur of wake up: murmur me down
that stream to the root: this incantation:
this *thank you, thank you, thankyousoverymuch,*
thank you.

She is in a crowded room, some sort of writing group or poetry reading. It is her turn.

She has either just composed the poem in her head moments before, or she makes it up as she goes along. Her delivery is hesitant, repeating certain lines for emphasis, especially the line about being right up against the edge of something. As she says those words, she feels herself literally pressed up on the edge. On the edge. On the edge. On the edge.

She finishes, the room is silent. Finally, one woman asks what kind of feedback she desires, but the tone of the woman's question implies that she doesn't know what to say about this poem, that none of the people do.

She wants to hide, but instead replies that it is raw writing, a first draft. The group starts to discuss the poem, and she is amused with their interpretation.

A man hands her a piece of paper on which she supposes he has written his feedback. There is a small waxed-paper baggie stapled to it. She opens the baggie and finds a collection of seeds.

The seeds fall into her hands—

Aubade for Sal

Oh, Shenandoah, I'm bound to leave you. Naked
on his back with legs and arms grasping
grasping air, grasping wild fear & flailing anger
grasping for his exploded desire. I climb
into Sal's bed and sing to him. I hold him
as he lunges for the window a last hope for escape
on this his last morning on earth.

I should let him jump through that portal
down into a stranger's backyard. I'll follow and we'll scale
the fence, cross the street to Berkeley Bowl grocery
where we'll buy his favorite double chocolate
chip ice cream and sit together on the curb
trading spoon back and forth, sweetness
slowly melting on our tongues. He will lick
the container clean, kiss me goodbye and saunter
whistling into the aubade of his afterlife
and I into my renewed materiality.

But I hold him back from that window. I seal
his final hours. I sing him *away*
rolling river I'm bound away as he invokes
Shakespeare and whispers Rilke and Ray Carver
I initiate the farewell kiss as he softens and slows
closes eyes & opens hands wide dropping
seeds of mo(u)rning into my waiting arms—
I press the seeds between these words
for safekeeping as Sal flies

out that window pulled upward *away*
rolling river away by beloved oracles of language
& I watch him fade toward distant
words—*How*

can all this weightlessness

survive.

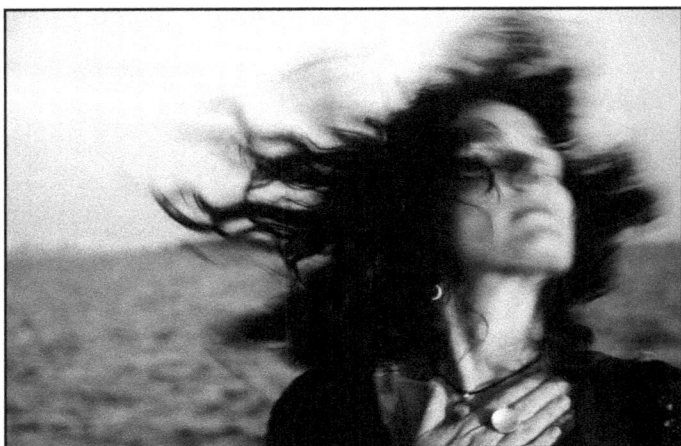

She watches wild horses. Huge, strong, and beautifully sleek, multi-colored horses that are most definitely untamed and free. They are almost dancing with each other & rearing up onto their hind-legs in an intricate give and take. Someone is trying to catch them, and she laughs, knowing that will not be possible.

Want

—after Michael McClure

From the beginning I am told:
I want is never a good enough
reason for anything. Words etched
into my ribs, words holding
an almost airless fire, a slow burn
husked hollow hunk of matter.
This is how my body becomes dust.

Yet today the tulips on the windowsill
curl toward light & heat with instinctive
want. The tulips curl into tendrils
into echoing lions of time
their dowsing & divining
tell me: Close your eyes & dive
into the deep end of clouds
where water moves through air
where want swirls & somersaults.

The tulips curl into my future self.
I see her there, walking the hills
old woman with glasses hazed
by breath, I watch her move
through translucence, the path
unclear. I watch that old woman
stop & stretch arms toward her wild
& solid self as she calls out—
This life, this life
is not what I expected.

Her perfect mammalian ghost roar.
Her desire.

ACKNOWLEDGMENTS

Alice Walker excerpts from the *Alice Walker in Conversation with Amy Goodman* event, Oakland, CA, January 27, 2006.

"Night Eats the Last of It" from *Velocity* by Nancy Krygowski, ©2007. Reprinted by permission of the University of Pittsburgh Press.

"Murmuration" first appeared in *sPARKLE & bLINK*.

Sal Salasin was a poet and the founding editor of *RealPoetik* ("oldest little magazine on the internet, publishing established and emerging poets since '96"). He died March 19, 2009, of lung cancer. The following poems contain his work:

March 10: excerpts from Sal Salasin, *Optima Suavidad*, Green Bean Press

The Brilliant Mr. Salasin: from *Stepping Out of the Plane Under the Protection of the Army*, Another Chicago Press

Aubade for Sal: the line How can all this weightlessness survive from the "The Brilliant Mr. Salasin"

Deep gratitude to Anita Barrows, Steven Black, Hollie Hardy, Kristin Prevallet, and Paul Corman-Roberts for sparking poetry in my life and in the world. And to Amanda, Rosie, Isaac: through everything you are my heart, my marrow. *Thank you, thank you, thankyousoverymuch, thank you.*

www.ingramcontent.com/pod-product-compliance
Lightning Source LLC
Chambersburg PA
CBHW050029090426
42734CB00021B/3474